S0-ASN-387

We Are All
Children
Searching
For Love

To Julie and Adam

I thank
whatever Gods may be
that you are well
and flying free

Leonard and Sandi Nimoy

Other books by

Blue Mountain Arts inc.

Come Into the Mountains, Dear Friend
by Susan Polis Schutz
I Want to Laugh, I Want to Cry
by Susan Polis Schutz
Peace Flows from the Sky
by Susan Polis Schutz
Someone Else to Love
by Susan Polis Schutz
I'm Not That Kind of Girl
by Susan Polis Schutz
The Best Is Yet to Be
Step to the Music You Hear, Vol. I
Step to the Music You Hear, Vol. II
The Language of Friendship
The Language of Love
The Desiderata of Happiness
by Max Ehrmann
Whatever Is, Is Best
by Ella Wheeler Wilcox
Poor Richard's Quotations
by Benjamin Franklin
I Care About Your Happiness
by Kahlil Gibran/Mary Haskell
My Life and Love Are One
by Vincent Van Gogh
I Wish You Good Spaces
by Gordon Lightfoot
Catch Me with Your Smile
by Peter McWilliams

We Are All Children Searching For Love

A collection of poems and photographs
by Leonard Nimoy

**Blue
Mountain
Arts** T.M.
Boulder, Colorado

Copyright © Leonard Nimoy, 1977.
Copyright © Blue Mountain Arts, Inc., 1977.
All rights reserved, including the right to reproduce
this book or portions thereof in any form.

Printed in the United States of America.

Library of Congress Number: 77-81666
ISBN: 0-88396-024-9
First Printing: August, 1977

Designed by SandPiper Studios, Inc.
Edited by Susan Polis Schutz.
Photo on page 63 Copyright © Leonard Nimoy, 197

Blue Mountain Arts inc.
P.O. Box 4549 Boulder, Colorado 80306

CONTENTS

Searching For Love

We Are All Children

Searching For Love

Thank you
For a world
of kindness

Thank you
For your endless
patience

Thank you
For your sensitive
understanding

Thank you
For your
Love

You fill me
    With your love

You fill me
    With your caring

You fill me
    With your thoughts

You fill me
    With your sharing

Because
    I have known despair
    I value hope

Because
    I have tasted frustration
    I value fulfillment

Because
    I have been lonely
    I value love

I am convinced
That if all mankind
Could only gather together
In one circle
Arms on each other's shoulders
And dance, laugh and cry
        together
    Then much
            of the tension and burden
                of life
        Would fall away
In the knowledge that
We are all children
Needing and wanting
Each other's
Comfort and
Understanding
We are all children
Searching for love

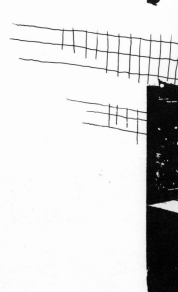

Love does happen
Like a touch
Of grace

It falls
Into place
Where there used
To be
Empty space

When I hold your
face
In my hands
I ask
How did this happen
To me?

When love happens
    Through a person or
    A song or a poem

What joy
    What excitement
To know that I
    All of me,
My child and my adult
    All of me,
Is touched again
    With the flowing love
    Of the best that is me
    And my fellow man
        That part of us . . .
            That cares.

You stepped
Deep into
The waters
Of my soul

Patiently you searched
For the precious
Stone

You found it
Warmed it
Caressed it
And gave it
To me
Unselfishly
As a gift

And now
It is ours
And we call it
Love

A silence with you
Is not
a silence

But a moment rich
with peace

Help me . . .

Help me
To say I love you
Because I do

It should be easy
To say I love you
Because
It's true

What is this fear
That ties my tongue
That locks
the words
away inside
deep inside

Help me
Turn the key

Help me
To speak
the truth . . .

Help me to say
I love you

Like a circle
    In the sand
Loneliness waits
    For a
        Love wind
To wash it
        To the sea

I'll be your
        wind
Will you be
        mine?

There is in me
A being little known
To others
A person,
     man or boy
Locked away

I believe
That he is me
More me
    Than the one
Anyone knows

And that he
Deserves at least
A trial
  Before being sealed away
Forever
  Locked inside
    The public face.

I am still a child

    Thrilled by a sunrise
    Touched by a bird-song
    Delighted by a clown

    Frightened by hatred
    Hurt by rejection
    Saddened by pain

Warmed by love

Now spend this day
        with me alone
We'll walk the beach
        and seek the stone
Which when it's found
        will wonders tell
            of magic lands
                and mystic bells
Of ships and sailors
        storms at sea
Of giant serpents
        swimming free

And you and I
        will know once more
        as we drift homeward
        from the shore,
            that we live in
A world sublime
        Two children
            In the strand of time.

Two beings meet
Stand side by side
Young and fearful
Protected by
Layer upon layer
Of defenses

Wanting
To reach
And be reached
Touch
And be touched
Wanting to open
And be opened

Time
  Joy
    Sorrow
      Fear
        all pass

And now
You tell me
I'm changed
Mellowed
Easier to be with

And so are you
        My child . . .
            So are you.

Go, my child
And find your way
Though I would rather
Have you stay

Take now your chance
To reach for more
Than ever I have known
Before

Add not your tears
To those men cried
In mourning
For their dreams that died

Look back, but now and then
To tell
Of where you go
And are you well

This thought to warm you
'gainst the chill
I love you now
And ever will

When I truly give
In a love
As the artist gives
In his art
I am fulfilled
Manyfold.

If I try
To make you believe
That all is good
And will be
    That would be a lie

    And a lie
    Stands between people
    As an invisible wall
    Denying closeness
        For fear that the lie
        Will spring out
        Into the open
            And attack . . .

A lie destroys trust
In oneself
And in each other

No,
    I will not try
    To have you believe
    That all is good

I am too selfish

    I want your love
    And your trust

We Are All Children

We are all children
   Seeking the fountain
We are all children
   Washed by the rain

We are the dreamers
   We are the dancers

Life is the music
   Love is the song.

We are all children
Needing laughter
Fighting tears
    Hiding fears

We are all children
Seeking release
Hungry for peace

We are all children
Crossing the ocean
We are all children
Tossed by the storm

Swimming the waters
Of God's devotion
Seeking a harbor to
Offer us home

We are all children
Of various ages

We are all children
The near and the far

Give us the peace
To search not for sages
Give us the strength
To love what we are.

Come,
    Let us dance together
          sing together.

Let us reawaken
      the innocence
      the wonder
      the simple
      Joy and faith
Which is rightfully ours

Let us unburden ourselves
    Of the disguises
      the roles,
      the weights,
      the chains . . .
Which hide and bind
The children
      That we are

For we are,
    All of us —
        Children.

We are the tree
          The leaf
          The bud
And the blossom

All are part
Of the fruit
Of God's love

Our love for one
Is our love
          For all

And if you take from me
I am blessed
For in the exchange
I am no longer
          Alone.

We are the players
And the game

We are the remembered
And the forgotten

We are the prize
And the loss,
The sweet,
And the bitter.
The accident
And the choice.

Each of us is Pawn
And King.

We are the miracle
   And the salvation

We are the expected
We are the past
      Present
            And always

We are the faith
   And the faithful

We are the leaders
   And the led

We are the masters
We are the slaves
 We are the beginning
  And the end

We are the storm
 And we are the calm
The ocean
 And the shore

We are each
 And we are all
We are every one
 The great
 And the small

We are the earth
We are the heavens

We are yesterday
  And tomorrow
We are the father
  And the son
  The giver
  And the given
There is no better
  And no worse

S____ us rejoice
          Let us sing
          ump,
                    Clap,
____nd dance to the music
For we are the music,
                    The words
                    And the dance

                    We are all.

"Find"

We are the poem
    And the poet
We are the words
    The paper
And the print

For we are here
    Together
In the circle
    Touching
And touched

We are the laughter
    And the tears

Who is it that sings?
    It is us
Who is it that cries
    Out?
It is us
    Who is it that
    Stumbles and falls
Then runs free
    In the field?
It is us

Then let us know it
    Let us drink it
Let us praise it
Let us savor it
    Let us thank each other

Let us ride the wave
To the crest
Of life

To take part
In the all
That we are

Let us sit on the
Top of the hill
in darkness
Watching and waiting
in the sure
And blessed
knowing
That the sun
which has been
Elsewhere
Visiting with
the others
of us
Will soon
be here
To warm our chill
To lighten our way

To embrace the all
That we are

Hallelujah

Let us give thanks
for the
Eternal spring
of love, Hallelujah!
Which is within us, Hallelujah!

The love we have
searched for
The love that is
ours
The love that is
The children
we are

Let us say
Hallelujah!
Amen

About the Author

If a man is measured by the various dimensions of his character, and by the integrity and love that are expressed in the fulfillment of each facet, Leonard Nimoy is surely one of the world's "special" people.

Most people recognize Leonard from his character role in television's Star Trek. But the millions of fans who think that they know Leonard Nimoy because they know "Mr. Spock" will discover an added dimension to Leonard's character within the pages of this book. However, the admiration and following that Nimoy has received as a result of his various roles attest to the fact that he is a superb actor.

Broadway, Hollywood, writer and director, singer and actor — the "public" Leonard Nimoy is an artist of the highest regard. In addition to being recognized as an educated and entertaining lecturer, Leonard feels at home in the roles of both teacher and student. After having taught at various acting schools and at Synanon for a time, he has recently completed his Master's Degree in education at Antioch College.

A glance at his credits and activities reveals the "public" side of Leonard — the side that is an extremely busy man, thriving on challenge, variety and professionalism. It has only been in recent years that the "private" Leonard Nimoy has emerged as a well known poet and photographer.

Ironically perhaps, Leonard's own poems and his richly creative expressions communicate more about the man than any observer could ever hope to say. Thematically, Leonard seems especially aware of our place in space and time, and his poetry often exudes an honest and open intimacy with everyman. On the other hand, Leonard's intense devotion to the special people in his life — people like his wife, Sandi, and their two children — instinctively shines through in shared and private moments. As a reflection of the man, the poetry and photography of Leonard Nimoy is interwoven with passion and compassion, a free-spirited sense of wonder and a deep, human sentiment.